A Growing Baby Sulcata
as told by
Elliott, the Sulcata

by Megan D. Nelson

Copyright © 2018 Megan D. Nelson

ISBN-10: 1724449346
ISBN-13: 978-1724449344

DEDICATION

This book is dedicated to Elliott who inspired this book, and to Dustin who always encourages me to venture wherever my passion leads me.

Hi! My name is Elliott. I am a baby African Spurred Thigh Tortoise (Sulcata). We are called that because we live in Africa and have spikes on the back of our thighs called "spurs". I hope you like my story.

It is hard being little. Everything is so big, and I am so small. One day, I will be 200 pounds and big enough to ride on, but right now, I fit in your hand.

On my first day with my new family, they made this enclosure for me to live in. It has everything I need inside. I will only live in this small space for a short time. I will grow very fast in the next few years.

I did not like my first time outside my enclosure.
I hid in my shell. The world is big and scary
sometimes. Are you ever scared? What do you do?
I pull my head in my shell and wait until it is safe
to move.

Look closely, I am hiding. Baby sulcatas like to dig and hide. In the wild, there are many animals that will eat little tortoises. This way, I can sleep and feel safe.

When I wake up, I stretch and bobble my head up
and down. I look at what is around me and check
if it is safe to move about.

Then, I eat! I love lettuce, especially kale and radicchio. The white specks you see on my food are calcium. Just like you need calcium for strong bones, baby tortoises need calcium for strong shells.

I also like blueberries! They are my favorite. In the wild,
I usually eat grass and hay. So, blueberries are a nice treat.

The blueberries are as big as my little head, but I can move them all over my enclosure. I am strong and amazing that way.

I like to walk, climb things, and move my feeding bowls to keep active. Sometimes, I will push a ball around.

I made a friend. He doesn't look too scary. Does he?
This is Porter. He is my dog friend. He watches over
me.

Someone thought it would be a great idea to play this big and loud cello by my enclosure. I am not sure how I feel about this.

Food is good for a lot of things. Sometimes, I like to use it for a pillow for my nap.

When I wake up, I take a dip in the pool. I will get a drink and cool off in there.

I went outside again. It was not so scary. It was actually really fun. I love to run through the grass and eat the sweet clover.

When I came back in, I was not very happy. I wanted to stay outside and play. Have you ever just wanted to stay out and play all day? When I am bigger, I will be able to stay out longer. I can't wait until then.

I was climbing around my pool, and I slipped and flipped on to my back. I laid there for hours, but I was rescued. Too much excitement today. I need a rest!

It might look like I am sleeping in my food dish, but look closely, I am watching you.

It's sleepy time, but first, I will take a dip in the pool.
Goodbye. See you next time, friends!

ABOUT THE AUTHOR

 Megan D. Nelson is a special education teacher, licensed behavior specialist, actor, and music instructor. When she isn't writing, performing, or teaching, she can be found running at local races and trails. She wishes to thank her son, Brandon, and her pets (Dakota, Cheyenne, Porter, and Elliott) for being an inspiration for her work, and Dustin for supporting her and contributing to this book.

Be sure to watch Elliott grow-up on Instagram at: "elliott _the_sulcata".